Weekly Bank Alert

Steps on how you can teach what you know to make 500-1000 dollars weekly,

Deborah Shepherd

Table of contents

How my journey started

It was a regular day and I found myself browsing aimlessly through the internet. Suddenly, the idea of teaching what I know online popped into my mind. I had always been passionate about my skills and I knew that I had the expertise to share with others. So, I decided to give it a try and created an online course on a popular learning platform.

The course was about the basics of graphic design and I put all my energy into creating materials that were easy to follow and informative. I recorded tutorial videos, designed exercises, and provided feedback to my students. I was committed to creating the best possible learning experience.

To my surprise, the feedback from my students was overwhelmingly positive. They loved my style of teaching and found my materials engaging. In just a few weeks, my course had hundreds of students enrolled and the money started rolling in.

The feeling of making my first $500 was indescribable. It was not just about the money, but also the validation of my skills and the satisfaction of helping others learn. From that moment on, I knew that online teaching was something I wanted to pursue further. It was an incredible experience that opened up new opportunities and allowed me to share my passion with the world.

Chapter 1

Introduction -Explanation of the idea of earning money through teaching - Benefits of this approach

Earning money through teaching is an increasingly popular approach for individuals looking to supplement their income or even earn a full-time living. This idea has gained traction due to the rise of online learning platforms, which have made it easier than ever for people to share their knowledge and expertise with a wider audience.

There are several benefits of earning money through teaching:

1. Flexibility: One of the biggest advantages of this approach is the flexibility it offers. Online learning platforms allow teachers to set their

own schedules and work from anywhere in the world. This makes it an ideal option for those who need to work around other commitments, such as a full-time job or caring for children.

2. Passive Income: Another advantage of teaching is that it allows you to generate passive income. Once you have created your course material or lesson plans, you can continue to earn money from them as long as people are interested in learning. This means that you can earn money while you sleep, travel or engage in other activities.

3. Personal Growth: Teaching can also be a rewarding experience that helps you grow as an individual. It requires you to think critically about your subject matter and find new ways to present the information to others. Additionally, teaching can help you develop communication skills, improve your own understanding of the

topic and gain a sense of fulfillment from helping others learn.

4. Low Investment: Starting a teaching business usually requires minimal investment compared to other entrepreneurial ventures. To get started,

all you need is a phone, computer, an internet connection, and some expertise in your chosen topic. This makes it an accessible option for people who may not have the financial resources to start a traditional business.

5. High Demand: There is a growing demand for education and personal development in our society. With the increasing number of people seeking to improve their skills and knowledge, teachers are in high demand. This means that there are plenty of opportunities to earn money through teaching, especially in niche areas where there is less competition.

Earning money through teaching is a viable and rewarding approach with many benefits. Whether you have a passion for sharing your knowledge or are simply looking for ways to supplement your income, teaching can be a lucrative and flexible way to achieve your goals.

Certainly! Earning money through teaching has become increasingly popular in recent years, thanks to the growth of technology and the internet. With online platforms like Facebook, Instagram, YouTube, Udemy, Skillshare, Etc. It's now possible for anyone with a skill, talent, or knowledge to create and sell educational content to students anywhere in the world.

One of the key benefits of earning money through teaching is that it offers a great deal of flexibility. You can create your own course or content and set your own schedule. You also have the freedom to teach from anywhere in the world, whether that's from the comfort of your own home or while travelling.

This approach can also be a great way to earn extra income or even make a full-time career out of teaching. If you are passionate and knowledgeable about a particular topic or subject, and you can communicate that passion and knowledge effectively, then there will always be people who are willing to pay for your expertise.

In addition, teaching can be a fulfilling way to share your skills and knowledge with others, and help them to achieve their goals. You might be helping someone to learn a new language, develop a new skill or even build a business. The sense of satisfaction that comes from seeing your students succeed can be incredibly rewarding.

Overall, earning money through teaching offers numerous benefits, including flexibility, potential for income growth, and the opportunity to share your knowledge and expertise with others.

Chapter 2

Identify Your Area of Expertise - Assessing your skills and knowledge - Identifying your passion

Teaching what you know is one of the best ways to earn money online. It is an excellent way to leverage your skills, experience, and knowledge to help others while also making a profit. However, before you start teaching, you need to identify your area of expertise.

Assessing your skills and knowledge is the first step in identifying your area of expertise. Start by making a list of all the skills and knowledge you possess in a particular field. Once you have identified your skills and knowledge, it's time to assess your expertise.

To assess your level of expertise, ask yourself a few questions. First, how long have you been involved in the field? Secondly, have you worked on any significant projects or have you received any recognition? Finally, how much success have you had in your field?

Identifying your passion is another critical aspect of identifying your area of expertise. Teaching what you know should be something you are passionate about. Teaching a subject that you are passionate about makes it easier for you to engage with your audience as you will be delivering your teachings with enthusiasm and commitment.

Teaching what you know is an excellent way to earn money online. It's essential to assess your skills and knowledge, identify your passion and leverage your expertise to help others while also making a profit.

In essence, teaching what you know involves sharing your knowledge and expertise with others who are interested in learning. With the rise of online learning platforms, it is easier than ever for anyone to become an online instructor and earn money by creating and selling courses.

There are several benefits to this approach. First and foremost, it allows you to capitalize on your existing knowledge and skills. Whether you are an expert in a particular subject, have specialized knowledge in a certain field, or possess a unique set of skills, teaching online is an excellent way to monetize your expertise.

Furthermore, teaching online allows you to work from anywhere at any time. As long as you have an internet connection, you can create and deliver content that students can access from anywhere in the world. This flexibility makes it ideal for people who want to work from home, travel, or have other commitments that require a flexible schedule.

Teaching what you know online can also help you build your brand and establish yourself as an authority in your field. As more people take your courses and benefit from your expertise, you can develop a reputation online that can lead to new opportunities and partnerships.

Chapter 3

Determining Your Target Audience - Defining your niche market - Understanding your potential students

If you want to be successful in teaching what you know, it is important to understand your target audience. This involves defining your niche market and understanding the potential students who may be interested in what you have to offer. Here are some tips to help you get started:

1. Define your niche market

The first step in determining your target audience is to define your niche market. This involves identifying a specific area of expertise that you are passionate about and creating content that aligns with it. Your content should be catered to a specific group of people who are interested in your niche market, making it easier to attract and engage potential students.

2. Understand your potential students

Once you have defined your niche market, you should work to understand your potential students. This involves researching their needs, preferences, and pain points to create content that addresses these elements. You can do this by conducting surveys, focus groups, or simply engaging with your target audience on social media or forums.

3. Create content that resonates with your target audience

Finally, it is important to create content that resonates with your target audience. Your content should speak directly to the needs and preferences of your potential students, making it more likely that they will be interested in what you have to offer. Use language and visuals that are eye-catching and engaging, and make sure that your content is informative, educational, and actionable.

In conclusion, determining your target audience, defining your niche market, and understanding your potential students are crucial steps to take when teaching what you know. By doing these things, you will be able to create content that resonates with your target audience, making it easier to attract and engage potential students while earning money doing what you love.

Chapter 4

Creating Your Curriculum - Developing course outlines - Setting learning objectives - Creating lesson plans

If you're considering teaching what you know, creating a curriculum should be at the top of your to-do list. Developing a curriculum is key to ensuring that your students receive high-quality education, and it is an essential aspect of creating a successful career as an online educator. Here are some steps you can follow to create your curriculum.

Developing Course Outlines

The first step in developing a curriculum is to create a course outline. A course outline should contain all the essential topics that you want to cover in your class. It acts as a blueprint for your course, and it helps you stay on track while creating your lesson plans.

Setting Learning Objectives

The next step is to set learning objectives. Learning objectives help you focus on what you want your students to achieve by the end of your course. Well-defined objectives enable you to create engaging and effective lesson plans that serve your students' needs.

Creating Lesson Plans

The final step is to create lesson plans. A lesson plan shows how you intend to teach each topic in your course outline. It specifies what you intend to do, how you plan to do it, and what materials you will need.

Creating a curriculum is an essential part of teaching what you know. By taking the time to develop a plan, you can ensure that your students receive the highest quality education and maximize your chances of achieving success as an online educator.

Creating a comprehensive and effective curriculum is crucial to the success of any teaching program, whether online or in-person. You may also want to use the following steps in developing a curriculum instead of the above:

1. Assess your expertise: Before developing a curriculum, it's essential to assess your skills and knowledge in the subject matter. Determining your capabilities and expertise will help you create a more relevant and effective curriculum.

2. Identify your target audience: It's important to consider your target audience when developing your curriculum. Their age, level of education, profession, and interests should be taken into account.

3. Develop course outlines: Create an outline for each course, which will include the course objectives, topics to be covered, and lesson plans.

4. Set learning objectives: Learning objectives are specific and measurable goals that you want your students to achieve. They should be clearly defined, achievable, and relevant to the subject matter.

5. Create lesson plans: Develop a lesson plan for each class session, which will include a detailed explanation of the expected learning outcomes, learning materials, and teaching strategies.

By following the above steps, you can create a comprehensive and effective curriculum that meets the needs of your target audience, and helps them achieve their learning objectives.

Chapter 5

Choosing the Right Teaching Platform - Different options for teaching, including online and offline methods - Factors to consider in selecting a platform

You need to choose the right platform to deliver your content, if you want to start teaching what you know. With so many options available, it can be overwhelming to select the best one to suit your needs. In order to make the most informed choice, consider the following factors:

1. Type of Teaching: The first step in choosing the right platform for teaching is deciding on the type of teaching you will be doing. Will you be teaching in-person, online, or a combination of both? Each platform has its own advantages and disadvantages, so it is important to identify which type of teaching will work best for your situation.

2. Target Audience: The platform you choose must accommodate your target audience. Are you targeting beginners or experienced learners? Do you want to focus on instructing kids or adults? Different platforms cater to different audiences, so it is important to consider this when making a choice.

3. Features: Look at the specific features offered by each platform. Do they offer easy video or audio recording? Is the platform user-friendly, and can learners easily access your content? Does the platform offer social media integration? These are all important factors to consider when selecting your teaching platform.

4. Cost: Determine your budget and look for a platform that fits it, but don't necessarily choose the cheapest option. You want to ensure that the platform you're using can effectively deliver

your content and help you reach your teaching goals.

By considering these factors, you can choose a teaching platform that suits your requirements and make the most of your time spent teaching.

Chapter 6

Developing Your Marketing Strategy - Creating a brand that reflects your area of expertise - Promoting your courses through channels such as social media, email marketing, and networking

Once you've created your curriculum and decided on your teaching platform, the next step is to develop your marketing strategy. Marketing your courses effectively will help you reach a larger audience, build your brand, and ultimately grow your business. Here are some tips to help you develop a marketing strategy for your teaching business:

1. Create a brand that reflects your area of expertise

Your brand should effectively communicate your area of expertise and the value you provide to potential students. Consider creating a logo, tagline, and defining your unique selling proposition (USP).

2. Develop a promotional plan

Create a detailed promotional plan that outlines the promotional channels you will use to promote your course. Social media is a powerful tool for reaching a broad audience. You can also create email marketing campaigns, leverage search engine optimization (SEO), and consider paid advertising.

3. Leverage your network

Networking can help you reach potential customers and partners in your field. By joining relevant groups, attending industry events, and connecting with colleagues and influencers, you can extend your reach and develop relationships that can be mutually beneficial.

4. Measure your results

Track your marketing efforts to see how effective they are. Use analytics tools to analyze website traffic, social media engagement, email open rates, and course enrollment. Use this data to adjust your marketing strategy and improve your results over time.

By developing a marketing strategy that incorporates these elements, you can promote your courses effectively and grow your teaching business over time.

Chapter 7

Pricing Your Courses - Researching and determining the appropriate price range for your courses - Understanding your target audience's budget

Once you've created your courses, the next step is to determine how much to charge for them. Setting the right price for your courses is critical to your success as an online teacher. Here are a few steps to follow when setting the price for your courses:

1. Research your competitors: Look at what your competitors are charging for similar courses. This will give you an idea of the standard pricing range for your courses.

2. Assess the value of your courses: Take a look at the amount of time, work and expertise you

have poured into creating your courses. This will give you an idea of the value of your courses.

3. Understand your target audience's budget: Consider your target audience's budget and whether the price of your course fits into it. You don't want to set the price too high and lose potential students who may not be able to afford it.

4. Determine your pricing strategy: Once you have an idea of your value and your target audience's budget, you can begin pricing your courses. You could either choose to price higher for a more exclusive and specialized audience or lower to cater to a more widespread audience.

However , pricing your courses is an important aspect of online teaching. By researching the appropriate price range and understanding your target audience's budget, you can set the right price that will attract and retain your students.

Chapter 8

Maximizing Your Earnings - Offering personalized coaching, consulting or mentoring to students for an additional fee - Upselling your courses by creating advanced level courses or offering a bundle

Once you've created your course, the next step is to maximize your earnings by offering additional services and products to your students. Here are two ways to do this:

1. Offering Personalized Coaching, Consulting, or Mentoring: By providing one-on-one sessions with your students, you can offer personalized support and advice based on their unique needs and learning style. This can be a highly valuable service for students who require additional help or who want to fast-track their learning.

2. Upselling Your Courses: Another way to maximize your earnings is to upsell your courses by creating advanced level courses or offering bundle packages. This helps students take their learning to the next level and provides you with additional income.

Overall, offering additional services and products is an effective way to create more value for your students while maximizing your earnings.

Chapter 9

Conclusion - Recap of the benefits of this approach - Encouragement to take action and start teaching what you know!

I never thought that I could make a living by teaching others what I know. But when I started sharing my knowledge and skills with my friends and family, I realized that I had a unique perspective and expertise that could benefit others. So, I took the plunge and started my own online teaching platform.

And it's been an incredible journey. The benefits of this approach are vast - not only have I been able to earn a living doing something I love, but I've also helped countless individuals reach their full potential. By sharing what I know, I've been able to make a meaningful impact on their lives and that's an incredible feeling.

I encourage everyone out there to consider teaching what they know. You might be surprised by how many people are interested in learning from you. Start by determining your target audience, creating a curriculum, and developing a marketing strategy. And most importantly, don't be afraid to take that first step. The rewards can be immeasurable, both personally and professionally.

In conclusion, teaching what you know can be a fulfilling and rewarding way to earn income while sharing your expertise with others. By following the steps outlined in this guide, including choosing your niche, creating a curriculum, Etc. The End